Breaking Into Light

LAURA MARTIN

Copyright © 2023 by Laura Martin

ISBN: 978-1-62429-443-3

All rights reserved. Portions of the book may be reproduced for personal or commercial use with credit.

Published through Opus Self-Publishing Services
Located at:
Politics and Prose Bookstore
5015 Connecticut Ave. NW
Washington, D.C. 20008
www.politics-prose.com / / (202) 364-1919

CONTENTS

Breaking Into Light

Introduction

What if we were to break—not apart into fragmentation, but into Light?

Breaking Into Light is a collection of poems that imagines this. This time is an apocalyptic backdrop of climate change, racial injustice, and the selling out of lives to the god of Profit. And too, this time is defined by those who work for the Good, who make beauty real, who stand outside in a summer night and listen. It is created with trees that bud during wars. It is made by those who choose recovery, or repair, or compassion. This book is meant to look at all that devastates, all that breaks, and to proclaim still that the greatest is always the Love.

Intended as a personal devotional and as a professional resource, these blessings are meant to travel. They are written to go with chaplains into rooms where outcomes are uncertain. They are written for pastors at gravesides or pulpits or in offering prayers. They are written for spouses waking up in empty beds after sixty years of marriage. They are written for the person who sits down to pray in a place where she never wanted to be. They are written for those who hear the news and don't know what to do next. They are written to proclaim that there is more than just present pain and future hope—that there is Spirit ever-with-us. And that there are wild angels whenever we look for them!

Wild Angels

Wild angels are my
favorite kind.
They have no idea where
they left their haloes,
and they let their robes
run through fresh mud.
They don't stand in formation
and sing with a choir.
Instead they show up and
change tires on highways,
sit down and have a beer
and listen,
trespass in the park
to sit on the swings
late at night.
They come to hospital rooms
to tell bad jokes,
to airports to carry
heavy bags,
to food pantries
when it's the end of the month
and the money has run out.
They believe in
Revelation unfolding,
in the sacred scripture
we write between
each other.

The Sacred Daily

blessing ordinary-extraordinary days

Alternate Headlines

Let your news be also
that peaches are ripe,
that a lost dog was found,
tired and wagging his tail,
and taken back home.
Let your news be also that someone
put a cool cloth on her mother's forehead,
that a man made fresh coffee for someone he loves,
that you can stand close to devastation and
also hear singing.
Let your news be that you are not required
to be happy,
yet you can still know joy.
Let your news be that someone has saved the card
you wrote her ten years ago,
or the words you gave him ten days ago.
Let your news be the Psalm that you remember,
the prayer you make as you move today,
the way you are not alone when you whisper
Amen.

Nothing Is Insignificant

When I say that nothing you do is
insignificant,
this is what I mean:
You, standing at the counter,
making pancakes for the person
you love,
matters.
You, turning to kiss his cheek
as you go together
into the cool white clinic
to get the test results you
already know will not be good,
matters.
You, standing at the door for
ten seconds longer,
to hold it for the next person,
who has not gotten the job, again,
matters.
This is not incidental.
This is the way that you
make the world.

In the Silence

My dog and I wake up
when it is still night
so we can sit in the color-dark
and listen.
He listens for the assured steps of the fox,
the early dogs and their people,
moving with intent,
for a rabbit near the yard.
I listen for Silence.
This is not the sound of absence
but the sound of so much presence.
This Silence shows me
stones rubbed smooth,
clarity,
enough.
This Silence gives me back
the breath I didn't know I was holding,
tells me I can get there
without moving.
This Silence is full
of everything I need to hear,
and I have to come back tomorrow
to hear and remember again.

For The Small

Remember that the world is
saved by small things.
Mustard seeds,
pieces of light
tangled through trees and windows,
enough.
Words given to you years ago
that find you again
in your kitchen,
when you are doubting your way.
The world is saved by
people who take ordinary things,
and use them for the good.
Your life is saved
by the way you remember
that grace can be so small,
you can trip over her
if you aren't paying attention.
Look again
and see.

A Blessing for our Bodies

May we learn to bless the bodies we have,
not the ones we imagine.
May we honor their limits,
and listen to what they say even when we
wish their reply was different.
May we be tender to what is changing
and aware of what holds.
May we let the word gratitude be an old quilt
around us as we give thanks,
not a common word at all.
Give thanks for hip bones and hands held,
for first breaths and last rites,
for seeing through a glass dimly,
but still seeing,
for the chance to feel tired
and complete.

Living Close

The world is too often charged by fear
and will disappoint you again and again.
Know this and go on anyway,
refusing to concede the good and the possible.
Let the voices of analysts keep silent today
and listen to the wisdom of rivers and trees instead.
There will be time for undoing and redoing,
but right now live close up to what and who you love.
Choose the book or the song or the apples baking.
Choose the sun coming through the window,
the dog completely satisfied as he sleeps,
the face of the person you love near you,
the letter you will finish writing.
Go back to the place where you found
honey coming from rocks
and take someone there with you.

For Dogs

Something in me
that I didn't know was traveling
came home when I found you.
Against our humanness that overcomplicates things,
you show us how to make a life:
Run when the possibility of it finds you.
Take joy, in bones or people or
in the sigh at night when you
circle to sleep.
Hold nothing back.
Play every day, with rainbow unicorns or old tennis balls
or the one who giggles and pretends to chase you.
Give away your heart
and keep your soul.
Believe that forever is this moment,
and that is enough.

Counting

To count your life,
count it by the single hour when you
watched your work across years
come together,
and understood then what it meant to strive.
Count it by the small hand you held
when she did something Brave,
and the way you remembered that you were
Brave too, if only sometimes.
Count it by the honeysuckle you found
and told no one about,
and count it by the secrets that you spoke
when silence needed to break.
Count it by what you were handed down,
and worked to undo before it
undid you.
Count it by the berries you ate when they
tasted of the sunlight that made them.
Count it by the way you learned
that you too were made through Light,
and fell asleep smiling in the dark.

“Teach me wisdom in my secret heart.”
-Psalm 51

Teach me to keep no grudges,
to open my hands,
to look for wild berries in summer.
Teach me to spend a day
counting nothing and
let me be changed by
what I find.
Teach me that rain and split light
are enough to make a sanctuary.
Let me bless not the ground
where I want to stand,
but where I do stand.
Teach me to doubt a hundred things
but not once the sound of your voice
when it speaks inside me,
so quietly I could miss
Your roar.

In This Day

It is worth saying again that
you will never finish everything–
the laundry, the sorting,
the giving of your entire heart
to another.
The most you can do this day is
lift up your eyes to the sky,
and remember that you are made
to be free under it.
It is to let your feet feel the ground,
and know that it holds you entirely as you are.
It is to look for miracles between your hands,
as common as salt.
It is to keep awake for grace,
which is always finding her way to you.

On Being Faithful

Let me not be faithful to the old stories
of people who used each other,
and claimed it was divine will.
Let it not be to the ways that only divide and exclude.
Let me be faithful to the tadpoles just born this morning,
moving in the water.
Let me be faithful to the birds who lift together into the sky,
and keep ascending.
Let me faithful to the tomatoes that grow all summer,
then stop when they are done.
Let me be faithful to the ones who say
they do not believe in God,
but rise every day to feed hungry people.
Let me be faithful to those who play music
with windows open,
and to those who have been devastated,
yet love.

Justice Denied and Justice Pursued

lament and calls to action

For You Know

For you know
Emmett Till,
Eric Garner,
Philando Castile
Ahmaud Arbery,
George Floyd.
For you know
the open casket,
stand your ground,
selling cigarettes,
Officer, I can't breathe.
For you know
the future, executed,
with witnesses present,
and the hope that has no pulse.
For you know
betrayal and silence,
it will stand up in court,
look away.
For you know
black mothers
beside graves,
lament,
the rose that is cut just to die.

These Stories Too

When you tell the stories
of this war,
tell these too:
tell of those who stand
under broken skies
and play music.
Tell of the women who will not leave
because cats cry for food
on streets near them.
Tell of the zookeeper who
sleeps next to his elephant,
saying calm words
when days tear apart.
Tell of those who take
what scant food they have,
and break it to share.
Tell of those who know that
Grace is real,
not from rumor of it,
but from encounter with it.

The Harder Way

It is easier to preach despair than Resurrection.
It is easier to destroy than to create.
It is easier to curse than to honor.
Choose the harder way.
Choose the way where dry bones rattle,
then find breath.
Choose the way where empty springs
become living water,
where the lost sheep
is carried home.
Choose the way of creation
in your hands.
Choose the way of healing
what is broken,
using whatever you have.
Choose the way of seeing
the seed that is yet to grow.
Sing to what you cannot
understand.
Go back and look again
and find the tomb
empty
and you, part of the rising.

Let There Be:
A Benediction for Right Now

Let there be light,
and gentleness,
and stuffed animals tucked into beds at night,
and coffee bought for a stranger,
and refugees welcomed at airports,
and alleluia on your lips
when you thought you had finished saying it.
Let there be those who study peace,
those who minister without books,
those who paint a world not yet seen.
Let there be those who take their pain and sing,
and those who take their hope and write.
Let there be grace so obvious
that you must stop to notice it.
Let there be those who trade disbelief
for daily bread.
Let there be all of us,
little benedictions
blessing something,
and not even knowing
all the places that blessing travels.

Remembering January 6th

On the day of Epiphany,
the Light made known,
the insurrectionists came with clubs,
telling the story of a myth
with no heroes.
On the same day that the
Magi paid homage to the baby
and the sheep let their sleep be thick,
the insurrectionists brought
bear spray,
zip ties,
and a gallows,
passing them off as gifts.
There was no singing to
go tell it on the mountain,
but only the held breaths
and prayers without ceasing
of those under attack.
There were the ones who
risked all to save
because they knew no other way.
Eugene Goodman,
Daniel Hodges,
Michael Fanone,
Harry Dunn,
Aquilino Gonell,

we remember your goodness.
And now we, hearers and tellers
of the story of Light,
remember that Epiphany means
Manifestation.
And what manifests from here is made
by our imperfect, human lives,
our collective choices,
and if we still, together, know the Light,
and go to the mountain to sing it.

It Has Been Left For Us

It has been left for us,
and we cannot buy stock in it,
or watch it outperform
market expectations.
We can only begin each day
seeking it again.
in the places within us
that remain
Still
against all that moves.
Cultivating it again,
from the promise of
seeds and broken things.
Making it again
from the ways that wars
have been ended too,
from the heroics acts
of sobriety
and truth-telling
and choosing another way.
Making it again with
what we find in our heart
and give away with our hands,
for it has been left for us.

-inspired by John 14:27 "Peace I leave with you; my peace I give to you."

What Rises

All things rise again.
I know that this is somehow true,
and do not need to understand the physics
to believe it....
Seeds in the ground,
the last moon of summer,
the prayer you whispered when there
was no one else in the room.
So pitch yourself toward what will not be finished
in the visible world.
Work for the seeds in the ground and the
birds that cannot yet fly.
Work for the home of the ones
not yet born,
and the ones whose bare feet have touched earth
for 100 years.
Work for what you thought you
had lost
and for what will not go unnoticed
by eyes other than your own.

The Lord's Prayer for Uvalde

Our God, who art
right here,
in Uvalde,
again,
after Buffalo,
after Sandy Hook,
after Virginia Tech,
after, after.
Hallowed be thy gunshot body.
Thy kingdom does not come today.
We give you this day our outrage
and our mourning.
Lead us not into the temptation of apathy
and resignation.
Deliver us from the evil of idolatrous prayers
prayed while children are given up
on altars built for guns.
For thine is the dying,
and ours is the doing,
and both of us meet in
the work of rising again.

A Poem About a War, and Its Ending

How do you write a poem about war?
Do you start with the little girl
crossing the soil that her grandfather loved,
holding her cat?
Or do you begin with the boys
conscripted into tragedy,
conviction not appearing on command?
Maybe you begin with the old men sheltering in subways
and the ones who have seen two wars already
standing guard outside.
Maybe you begin in the basement of the hospital
where nurses rock babies,
blessing beyond religion.
Maybe you begin with a President who values
the sound of democracy more than
his own living voice.
But of course the question is never really
how do you begin a poem about war,
but always "how does it end?"
It ends when everyone–
the little girl,
the conscripted soldiers,
the old men,
the babies,
the nurses,
the President–

can lie down under our shared stars,
and sleep,
then wake to sunflowers growing.

Liminal Spaces

between what has been and will be

(for transitions)

If You Are

If you are angry, let your anger be fire
so it can warm someone chilly.
If you are grieving, let your grief be a river
so someone thirsty can drink.
If you are numb, let your numbness give you capacity
to walk in hard places and not feel hurt.
If you are broken, let your brokenness
be what makes space for a new thing to enter.
If you are fearful, let your fear be a warning signal
that others may look up.
If you are lost, let your being lost
make a new place and call it home.
However you are,
keep going.
However you are,
keep going.

More Than Fear

Maybe the line is not so much "do not fear,"
but do not stop at your fear.
Some days you will serve it tea,
sit down and listen.
Some days you will take it into your arms
and rock it over your shoulders.
Some days you will let it have its tantrum in front of you,
and other days you will debate it
until you both fall asleep.
Let yourself be afraid, then,
but not only that.
Let yourself be afraid, then,
but also receive what comes in
through the slants of sun,
or the space open for you.
Let yourself remember
that the end of a hard road
is a new place,
and you only go there
by moving.

What It Looks Like When I Pray for You

Sometimes it looks like a river rock
held in my hand and then
returned to water.
The water ripples, then stills,
and I remember that the ripples
existed.

Sometimes it looks like evening turning to night.
Then I too fold up the light,
and let it rest from all it has done,
trusting it knows when to return.

Sometimes it looks like an old quilt,
softer from time, understanding.
How did we ever want something that wasn't soft?
There is always room for your secret from third grade
or the way you mourned yesterday when no one saw.

Sometimes it looks like a hallelujah said to the pine trees,
like a new beginning for an old story,
like both of us staying up all night
talking without having to say
anything,
and hearing everything.

Let Nothing Be Wasted

Let nothing be wasted.
Use everything--
the night you woke up, afraid,
the time you understood joy
as a living thing,
the day you took a risk,
and lost,
but were not defeated.
Because you have known
what it is to feel alone
standing under stars,
meet another there.
Because you have known
what is it to be cold
and have someone put a sweater on your shoulders,
do likewise.
Because you have known
how the sublime can find you
when you cut a lemon,
touch a tree,
kiss a forehead,
give this away too.
Let nothing be wasted.

On Change

Expect everything to turn.
The geography of your face will change,
and the feel of sun on it
in different seasons.
The ways you say yes will change,
and why and how you do.
The ground that feels steady
will start to move,
and will move you.
Honor what is secure in its insecurity.
Honor what evolves,
what leaves something behind,
what makes a new language
from a fragment of a word.
Remember that Resurrection too
only happened through change.

Practice Undoing

Practice disappointing someone else
if it keeps you upright in this torn world.
Practice being deliberate with your heart,
trusting her instinct and intention.
Practice gentleness with yourself---
beginning, middle, end.
Practice creating what stirs Beauty
that only you can see.
Practice the way of slow,
of this breath,
of right here,
of amen,
which means,
"So be it."

Priority List

Know today all you cannot repair,
So that you are free for all you can.
Let a hundred things be left undone,
For you to do the one that matters most.
Maybe you will cross a stream and look for what lives in it.
Maybe you will cross the expanse of your spirit
And look for what lives in it.
Maybe you will be there when the cardinal comes to drink,
or the eyes of someone you love turn to your face.
Maybe you will grow something or harvest something.
Maybe you will make a stitch or let a prayer rise.
These are no simple acts.
This is your foundation.

In This Day

Gaze not too far ahead as you walk,
which is why we pray,
"Give us this day, our daily bread."
Know that you will be offered work
that is not yours to do.
Know that you will carry something heavy
because you must.
Travel though you don't have all the answers.
Let yourself navigate by stars that you cannot name,
but trust.
Find the horizon within,
and see that
you are held in grace,
even if grace is beyond your comprehension.

Home By Another Road

This was not where you intended to be, or how.
The re-routes and surprises, the lost hours,
the night that cracked open with you in it.
This, then, will be the way you go.
So go listening for the way your name
is still said with softness.
So go with your hands cupped to hold
what strangers give you as you pass.
So go with your eyes tilted up to
the blue promise a tent above you,
and go with your feet sure-footed,
knowing this new ground holds you too.

On Shattering and Strength

The world will always try to sell you something
for your insecurity.
Laugh at this.
Believe that the strongest part of you is
also the place that has broken,
and more than once.
Remember the myth that says
the light shattered, and we are invited
to spend our lives collecting it again.
Remember that if anything is too heavy to carry,
it is because you try to carry it alone.
Remember the way a bulb lives quietly all winter,
then rises, saying
the answer was yes all along.

Grief: Yours, Mine, and Ours

for shapes of grief

Night Hymn

I listen to the night's hymn--
Katydids, crickets, cicadas.
There will be silence
when the first hard frost kills them all
in a night.
Learning this,
in this year,
undoes me.
There are no small griefs.
So let yourself grieve the silence
that will not be broken by your favorite voice.
Let yourself grieve the moment that you waited for
that did not arrive.
Let yourself grieve the abrupt ending,
the movement without direction,
the fruit that fell and did not ripen,
the night when you looked up
and saw no stars.
Know that Grief, Herself,
holds you and feels too.

For Those Who Died From COVID

Take the number
and multiply it by the
times they fell in love.
Multiply it by the cups of hot coffee
they drank with friends
across wooden tables.
Multiply it by the summers they stood
barefoot on sand,
fell asleep with windows open
to the conversations of katydids and crickets.
Multiply it by the nights they noticed
a chill in the air, and put a blanket around
someone else's shoulders.
Multiply it by the omelets flipped,
the garlic chopped in a kitchen
while the light came in.
Multiply it by the fires built
when you didn't know if the flame would take.
Multiply it by the stars you saw together.
Multiply the good.
Multiply the grief.
Multiply the way you
count all that is lost.

Remembering

I want to tell you that
the leaves stayed green on the trees this year
for longer than I thought possible.
I want to tell you that
the way you held my hand
made me feel safe and protected,
and the way you let it go, trusting,
made me feel capable.
I want to tell you that I believe in
the good, the possible, and the sacred
because you showed me how they are real.
I want to tell you that I hold on to words
you gave and seeds you made grow.
I want to tell you that I remember the
small moments,
which of course I know now are not small,
but everything.

From First Grief

In my first real grief,
I wanted to flee.
I wanted to go west from its east,
go south from its north.
I wanted to take the shortest route
pointing away.
Now there are times that I stop
in a full downpour,
in the desert that
gives us water too.
Now there are times that
I feel the drenching
and know that is all another way
that Love calls for us.

All In the World

For all that is in the world
that devastates you,
there is also this---
the dog who
leans his body against yours,
and exhales.
The way that katydids make sounds
on summer nights
by raising their wings.
The way that the basil grows strong
and green.
The way that we too
have strength,
(Yes, you do)
and attention,
and the choice to
mark what matters to us.

The Last Night

On the night before we die,
we may not get to gather with our friends in a room.
We may not get to proclaim
our leaving and mark ways for them to remember us.
On the night before my father died,
he drew logos for a political campaign
and called a neighbor about a magazine subscription he was getting.
The magazine came with a free football jacket,
and he thought that she knew someone who would want the jacket.
In the nights before my grandmother died,
she ate peach ice cream for dinner,
and clapped at the nurses who cared for her
because she knew they liked that.
Perhaps we would not want that last night
with all its attendant pain and shadowy foreknowledge
and the stakes so high that
everyone is afraid to be funny or irreverent,
when sometimes those things are most needed.
We don't know how much of our circumference of time
we've already walked,
or what diameter of laughter and pleasure,
grief and grace,
is still ahead to meet us.
Perhaps then we can mark our time,
all the time,
that others may know the ways they claim our hearts
and mark us too.

A Particular Grief

Maybe today you will grieve
his fingers playing keys on a piano,
the feel of him standing in a room with you.
Maybe you will grieve the
words you shared---
like trust, and prayer, and cinnamon,
and the way you rested together,
when neither of you needed words.
Maybe today you will grieve
the lemonade in her hands,
the light in her kitchen,
the way she taught you how to knead dough,
your story in the world told because of
who you were with her.
Maybe today you will grieve the absence of
your cat in your lap,
self-possessed and on his terms.
Or the way no dog presses her warm body
into you now,
remembering her tail that could not stop wagging.
Let memory, grief, grace all in.
The love hasn't ended.
The Love hasn't ended,
it has just changed forms,
and continues,
and not just
in you.

What Can Be Given

I cannot give you the moon's prayers,
or the path that leads back to a home
that no longer exists.
I cannot give you relief from longing,
assurance of ease in your days,
trust that your steps will be safe.
But you can go out and find
honey from a rock.
You can drink the cup of water
that has become wine
when you were not looking.
You can rest your feet
in a stream in the desert,
know awe,
taste manna,
take direction from a star inside yourself,
and live.

To Everything There Is A Season

for the turning in the year, liturgical and secular

To Everything There Is a Season

I have stood in this place and watched the light
on a July evening.
And I did not call the light here,
and I did not summon it away.
I have known the taste of strong coffee,
and sweet fruit still wet from rain.
I have lost something that had meaning,
and I found it again in another form,
but still grieve the first.
I have known awe,
and whimsy,
have been tired by the right things,
and stood too close to the wrong ones.
I have been disillusioned,
then looked back and saw the scene change.
I have seen a hummingbird feed,
and a dog run through snow,
a man breathe his last
in a room with full sun,
and spring return when I had
forgotten that there could be cherry blossoms.

For Christmas Eve

We come again to the manager tonight and look,
finding straw, stars, astonishment.
We feel the fur of animals who know that
the journey is not done,
but tonight, they pause here.
Tonight we pause here.
Tonight, we remember
that Mary said yes to God not knowing what
would come next,
trusting in what could not be seen.
and we find in her yes,
in the baby,
in the straw, stars, astonishment,
our own lives, too—
uncertain but marked even now by grace.
We remember that this night is birth of the One
who would grow up and take salt, and figs, and human longing,
and tell us this was all holy.
Who would take justice, and deliberate mercy,
and the memory of his mother singing to him,
and tell us that is what makes the world.
Who would take nets in the water, and broken bread,
and wilderness moments,
and say nothing in our lives is wasted.
Who would take water,
and promises,

and love that unfolds and flies,
and tell us that these things always live.
We come again to the manager tonight and look,
finding straw, stars, astonishment.
and as we look we realize that our voices
have always been enough to speak of this love.
Through our voices,
and our uncertain lives,
and grace,
in straw, in stars, in astonishment,
this Love was born,
is born,
will be born yet again.

Ash Wednesday

And when I go back to dust,
ash,
and earth-song,
I hope that the ashes remember the fire that caught to make them.
I hope they remember the singing that was all around them
I hope that they articulate again all of the light
that swayed inside for so long.
And I want to think now too
of how the ashes are inside me already.
May the ashes let me
remember and forget,
keep silence and speak out,
seek justice and claim mercy,
and see another's face and
remember their ashes too.

Eastering, This Year

Do not be so sure of how the story goes
that you miss it happening.
Again or still—it does not matter.
Even Mary did not recognize him at first,
thought him to be the gardener.
So resurrection comes in not just
one form.
The bird
returns home, descending.
Something caught in you,
unsaid for seasons,
is wrenched free.
You don't have to know the Source
to see the movement.
Fire poppies
germinate with the smell of smoke
and bloom in ashes after the burning.
You fall backwards,
realize that resurrection can be
what lets you see
what you never had before.

For Pentecost

Pentecost us this day,
that we might again believe in each other.
Give us future memories of
the day we learned to speak
a new language,
and let go of the old words
that kept breaking in the same places.
Teach us to pick up alleluias
on the sand where we walk,
in the grass where we
lie down next to someone
who makes us laugh,
in the company of revolving planets.
Release us from speaking any amens
out of obligation,
so that we can say yes to the ones we believe.
Show us how to make an alphabet
from peonies,
and found light,
and the way we were once hungry,
then fed.

Let Your Heart Be

Let your heart be troubled.
Let your heart be troubled by all that points away
from Life,
that stands on the street and
sells it out for 30 pieces of silver, still.
Let yourself be struck by grief,
lost for days,
fallen,
left without words.
Let yourself be angry, without apology.
Let yourself feel all of it.
This troubling is holy too, says the One who
broke apart the world.
Let your heart be.
And then let your heart find rest
in the curve of grace,
in the space of the undone.
Let your heart find the place
where you and Mystery meet, dancing,
on a warm enough night,
or at the day's rising, watching tree and leaf blow.
Let your heart find rest in the washing of the dish,
in the walk with the dog.
Let your heart find rest in a voice remembered,
or a letter written.
Let your heart find rest in thank you and amen,

in the ordinary and the sacred,
and the way these two are always meeting.
Let your heart be.

-inspired by John 14:1: "Do not let your hearts be troubled.
Believe in God, believe also in me."

Seasons of Presence

There are days I walk and feel
the ruin of each leaf under me.
There are days I look for blossoms and find
only bare branches.
There are days when I want my God
to be one of neat silence.
But then, without my doing anything,
some unsummoned Beauty
comes before me.
Night splits and flickers into first light,
or the bird finds her seed,
or the dog bounds home.
I know then that everything is fragile
and that everything does not have to last
to be eternal.

What I Wish For You

I wish for you candles and times to light them,
summer nights when you forget your calendar,
an understanding of what it is to trust.
I wish for you connections that you can pick up after years,
as though the conversation only paused,
and now you resume.
I wish for you places where you can laugh,
anticipation,
the presence of real grace.
I wish for you friendships with those
who tell you more about who you are
than you would know on your own.
I wish for you extravagance of time,
prayers prayed when you didn't realize
you were praying.
I wish for you
grounded hope
and room for you and the incomprehensible
to walk together.

Blessing For The End Of This Year

This year too, butterflies flew thousands of miles,
Hummingbirds ate enough,
People were saved.
This year too, men planted roses,
Women wrote novels,
People left relationships that made them doubt themselves.
This year too, parents spooned applesauce into infant's mouths,
And adults fed their parents in beds with old quilts.
This year too was marked by
What has always held the world--
Tenderness,
Sacrifice,
The luminous,
And you, still in it.

First Leaf

When the first leaf turns red you say,
"It's early, this year."
Yet to the leaf, it was simply
On time.
Why wouldn't you give this
To yourself too?
What have you also wanted to do,
And kept yourself from doing?
The timing is your own, too,
So turn,
Color.

Dedication

To Charlie, for everything. In your company, night never arrives. Your love is the honor of my life.

To Dale, without whom this book would not exist. Because of you, I kept writing. Because of you, I kept imagining this book into being. Thank you.

To Kathy, for believing in what could not be seen, and harvesting Light. I am continually in awe.

To Melissa, for always showing up in love, even when it is not easy or convenient, and for still standing close to laughter.

To Sara, for looking for the good, honoring the possible, removing the invasives, and reading all of life beside me.

To Parke, for who you are and how you are. The world is better because of your presence in it.

To John, for your faithful ways of showing people how beloved they are. Is there a greater calling?

To Karen, for honoring all that lives and all that gives life.

To Jessica, for knowing how to do everything so well, especially friendship.

To Nora, for pigs and poems and the way my face hurts from laughing after being with you.

To Jessie, for talking Rilke and angels and harvests seen and unseen.

To Sathi, for teaching me to be half-opened, half-closed, and exchanging false hope for present hope, found closer than I first thought.

To Pam, for saying yes to me so long ago, and yes to me in so many ways since then.

To Ashley, for administering the sacred and the real and living with the contradictions.

To Elizabeth, for caring deeply. Your voice echoes long after you stop singing.

To Ed, for playing more than just notes.

To Sarah, for the way tenacity and compassion meet in your life.

To Kathryn, for catching the words spoken and unspoken.

To Josh, for helping us all to hear the Music.

For Hannah, for beginning with attention and compassion.

To Matt, for the way you continue the Song you've heard all your life, and for your belief in me.

To Andrew, for making your weeks matter, for too much, and for what does not need to be said.

To Jill, for knowing that what is hard and what is beautiful live side by side, and for the ways you show up in grace for all of it.

To Mom, for waterfalls and encouragement.

To Ana, for always cheering me on.

To the congregation of Rock Spring United Church of Christ--you are all ministers to me.

To my dog Finn, for teaching me to romp and pay attention to joy.

Printed in the USA
CPSIA information can be obtained
at www.ICGtesting.com
JSHW080731121023
49836JS00003B/11